Step By Step Guide

1. Read the main scenario introduction
This sets up the overall context and central challenge you are facing.

2. Choose one of the presented options
There will be 2 options laid out at the end of the intro scenario, each with an assigned page number. Read these and select the one that aligns best with how you would like the story to unfold.

3. Turn to the page number listed by your selected option
Flip ahead in the story to the page number that your chosen option instructed you to visit. Here you will find a continuation of the tale based on the path you selected.

4. Evaluate the new scenario details and next options
Assess the new details that emerge as a result of your initial option selection. Then scan the revised options presented, which will branch the story in new directions informed by your previous choices.

5. Repeat steps 2-4 as needed
Each option will send you to a new page revealing fresh details and subsequent options that build on prior elections. Repeat this process, choosing options and turning pages until you reach a concluding chapter.

6. Arrive at your customized ending
Eventually your selections will lead to a customized ending tailored around the specific narrative path your options created. Congratulations, you successfully completed a "Prompt Your Own Adventure" story! Now go back and try the next main scenario.

Table of Contents

Code Development

As CS Solutions' star engineer, you've been picked to spearhead development of a sophisticated intrusion detection system for Third National, a major financial institution with an impenetrable cybersecurity mandate.

This high-stakes project represents a linchpin in CS Solutions' expansion into the lucrative financial sector. But with Third National's nonnegotiable deadline just weeks away, the pressure threatens to overwhelm. Do you dare take a calculated risk by letting an experimental AI algorithm generate the first pass at the code? Or stick to tiresome human habits, even if it means crunch time agony as the deadline looms?

Option 1: Sufficiently wowed by GenAI's code-writing capabilities in your personal projects, you decide to discreetly use tech to fast draft the detection system's first version. You rationalize that no company policies forbid this handy shortcut. ***Go to Page 25***

Option 2: Keenly aware that Third National entrusted CS Solutions' due to your engineers' superior judgment, you cannot justify compromising your reputation by testing unproven GenAI. So you grit your teeth and settle in for long nights manually coding the intrusion system line, determined to prove carbon still rules. ***Go to Page 21***

Job Hunt

The cutthroat tech industry has claimed another victim – you. As you numbly pack your desk into a cardboard box, the data science skills that once made you a hot commodity suddenly seem obsolete overnight.

Weeks pass in a blur of dead-end applications met by silence or, even worse, overly peppy rejection bot replies. Just as desperation peaks, your ex-colleague Zain swears he's cracked the code to creative AI-powered resumes that "Wow recruiters and guarantee interviews." Could this be your lifeline back into the field you've spent years cultivating expertise in?
Do you...

Option 1: Cautiously test the waters by feeding your tired old resume into Zain's résumé assistant bot for an optimization refresh. The AI engine restructures content to spotlight relevant skills and align your experiences with industry trends. Even slight polishing could give your job search that vital edge! *Go to Page 14*

Option 2: Decide it's time to go all in! You give the bot access to your full work history details along with old resumes. Let artificial intelligence work its magic to reinvent you as the ideal candidate and land your dream job in one fell swoop! *Go to Page 37*

Legal Conundrum

You are a savvy lawyer thriving in the world of high-stakes legal battles. But your newest case could be your greatest challenge yet. Your loyal client Maria Rodriguez – an entrepreneur with big dreams – built her latest startup "LocalLink" after her disastrous split from business partner Alan Mitchell. But Alan unexpectedly slammed Maria with allegations of stealing his prized proprietary AI algorithms for her app.

With Maria's livelihood on the line, you rush to your downtown office to prepare a counterattack. Sifting through Alan's claims, you realize his formidable legal team intends to crush Maria with everything they've got.
In this David and Goliath showdown, Maria is counting on you to save the day. Do you stick to tried and true legal sparring? Or fight fire with fire with your own AI-powered arsenal? How you fight could determine if LocalLink lives or dies!

Option 1: Employ a cutting-edge GenAI tool to analyze the legal details, automatically summarize the key issues, and draft a compelling response emphasizing the distinctions around AI-created algorithms. *Go to page 15*

Option 2: Personally write a case summary, then refine your arguments by running them through a GenAI system, ensuring a persuasive impact. *Go to page 22*

Professor

As a tenured history professor at Ivy League bastion Wellington University, you've reached icon status through bestselling books and award-winning classes. However, rumblings of "dusty tradition" hound you as the administration pushes modern GenAI integration.

Though hesitant to tamper with time-tested teaching methods, you know evolution is key to enduring relevance. So you embark on a quest to judiciously weave silicon enhancements into your course's fabric without compromising the sanctity of scholarly wisdom honed over centuries.

Seeking fresh perspectives, do you:

Option 1: Consult your star TA Alex, a pedagogical prodigy brimming with ideas on fusing AI's potential with human insight to uplift students. Their cutting-edge suggestions could modernize your approach while retaining its soul. *Go to Page 28*

Option 2: First dip your toes into automation by deploying AI to handle the deluge of administrative minutiae from students. Offloading robotic replies for common inquiries could free you to focus on higher pursuits. *Go to Page 11*

Financial Analyst

After acing quantum physics models predicting profitable trades by factors once deemed unquantifiable, your reputation as Quantitative Finance Solution's most ingenious wunderkind precedes you. Yet as you're called into the executive wing for your loftiest role yet, a palpable tension in the air implies something immense weighs in the balance.

"Your pioneering talent is perfectly suited to lead our boldest foray yet into algorithmic financial AI," the CTO declares. "If successful at unlocking market insights beyond the perceptions of mere mortals, you will usher this company into a stratosphere only your brilliance can envision." Buoyed but daunted as the Keys to the Kingdom land in your grasp, the options become starkly clear:

Option 1: Trust no one but yourself, deciding to hand-code a custom deep learning algorithm from scratch, finely tuned to your specification. The solo quest is daunting, but victory would cement your genius mythology. *Go to Page 16*

Option 2: Conclude these challenges require collaboration with seasoned experts. You recruit an acclaimed AI firm, leveraging their years of specialized experience in training market predictive models on complex multivariate data. *Go to Page 23*

Medical Research

Your peers acknowledge you as one of the visionaries pioneering biomedical research into rare diseases. Now, as a researcher at trailblazing BioPharm Innovations, you spearhead development of a groundbreaking new drug offering hope to patients in dire need.

Years of data gathering are finally complete, with petabytes tracking the experimental compound's efficacy. Your analysis will dictate if the drug progresses to final clinical trials - or languishes unfinished.

Faced with massive datasets transcending human processing capability, do you?:

Option 1: Entrust an award-winning AI system to conduct the expansive number-crunching, trusting its pattern finding algorithms to accurately determine if the drug demonstrates adequate patient benefit versus risk. Its insights could propel a medical revolution - if correct. *Go to Page 69*

Option 2: Insist on personally analyzing the mountain of statistics by hand first. With lives at stake, you cannot risk overlooking subtle clues only human intuition may detect in the data that silicon processors might miss. *Go to Page 17*

HR Manager

As HR trailblazer at red-hot a startup Amplify, you've been tasked with the most high-pressure recruitment of your career - a visionary Head of Marketing capable of turbocharging growth trajectories ahead of the impending launch of the company's revolutionary product.

Turning with temptation towards AI generative technology, you wonder if computational linguistics beyond mortal scope could manifest the perfect job description to reel in the finest creative talent at machine speed. The options stand:

Option 1: Turn the AI loose to fully construct the marketing role description from scratch. Unbounded, its computational creativity could reel in Silicon Valley's mostoutside-the-box unicorn executives if tuned right. ***Go to Page 18***

Option 2: First pen a detailed draft yourself outlining candidate must-haves tailor-made for your vision, then fine-tune it using AI to sculpt more compelling and broader appeal. A balanced combo of human and machine could create magic.
Go to Page 26

Marketing Campaign

After years striving as an associate, your hard work is rewarded with an appointment as team manager right as the firm wins its biggest account - launching a new "healthy soda" from client NaturalElixir.

As the creative briefing approaches, the pressure builds. This campaign could make or break the firm's reputation as a partner leveraging leading-edge tech. The team assembles looking to you for direction. "Alright folks, let's start...brainstorming!"

Option 1: You opt for a direct approach, inputting campaign details into a cutting-edge generative AI server, and requesting potential taglines. Here are some of the suggestions:

1. Revitalize Your Thirst!
2. Open Joy
3. Elevate Your Hydration with [Brand Name]
Go to Page 12

Option 2: Acknowledging the importance of a holistic campaign, you input the campaign details into the generative AI server, requesting themes and taglines.

1. Theme: Nature's Symphony in Every Sip
- Harmony in Health: NaturalElixir
2. Theme: Sparkling Wellness for Every Occasion
- Celebrate Life with NaturalElixir's Bubbly Goodness
3. Theme: Discover Your Freshest Self
-Uncover Your Best with NaturalElixirs's Refreshing Choice

8   ***Go to Page 41***

Travel Plans

As travel agent at idyllic Paradise Resort, you craft once-in-a-lifetime experiences - but the daily barrage of guest inquiries threatens to overwhelm you. Between juggling a perpetually overflowing inbox, phone ringing off the hook, and coordinating endless logistics, you are struggling to keep up.

Late one night, struggling to respond to yet another "Which yoga retreat package is right for me?" email, it hits you - AI automation could liberate you from these mundane tasks!

Option 1: Build an AI chatbot to handle the torrent of guest inquiries, bookings, and resort info questions. Automating these rote interactions could free you to focus on higher-level planning. ***Go to Page 32***

Option 2: Input resort offerings into a generative AI, asking it to create sample guest itineraries for review. Outsourcing tedious trip planning legwork could allow you to focus on refining vs churning itineraries. ***Go to Page 20***

CEO

As decade-spanning CEO of heritage manufacturing stalwart Rockwell Industries, your balanced leadership blending tradition with strategic innovation has navigated changes in the tide...until now.

In a routine leadership meeting, your whip-smart but youthful new manager Sara effusively evangelizes integrating "GenAI" - apparently some newfangled technology - to accelerate operations. Sara volunteers you to pioneer implementing this perplexing GenAI to exhibit its potential for modernization.

Nodding vaguely to mask utter unfamiliarity with this buzzword, you swerve discussion to safer ground. But Sara's expectant stare implies action is required. Back in your office, what now?

Option 1: Choosing to fake comprehension to avoid embarrassment, you vaguely assure Sara you'll "look into" his AI thing without intention to actually investigate further. No sense learning new tricks for an old dog like you! *Go to Page 29*

Option 2: Resolving to understand these mysterious modernizations before leading any rollout, you privately research exactly how GenAI could impact everyday decisions at Rockwell - from schedules to neckties! Once oriented, you can strategically steer integration. *Go to Page 13*

Professor

Inundated by endless administrivia, you find student emails dragging you away from scholarly pursuits. To reclaim precious time lost to questions about deadlines or grade minutiae, you design a GenAI system to auto-generate common replies.

Soon it actively fields the torrent of logistics questions, freeing you from robotic responses. With the newfound mental space this provides, thoughts inevitably turn to how else GenAI could elevate education beyond secretarial duties...

Option 1: Delegate your star teaching assistant Alex to spearhead exploring innovative integrations like AI-enhanced lessons. Their passion for the future of ed-tech could uplift your partnership to new heights. *Go to Page 28*

Option 2: Take the leap yourself into increased automation by trusting pretrained algorithms to generate your upcoming midterm exam. This trial by fire will reveal if silicon teachers can match carbon expertise at the core of scholarly evaluation. *Go to Page 48*

Marketing Campaign

You opt to input the campaign details into your firm's state-of-the-art generative AI server, requesting potential taglines to convey the client's desired messaging. The AI swiftly returns selections like: "Revitalize Your Thirst", "Open Joy", and "Elevate Your Hydration with NaturalElixir". After careful consideration of the options, you decide "Open Joy" best encapsulates the spirit of the creative brief from the client.

This tagline will serve as a promising starting point. But key decisions remain regarding how to expand this into a full integrated campaign. Do you:

Option 1: Energized by "Open Joy", you call an impromptu team huddle to collaboratively riff on the theme. Your group mines the phrase for symbolic meaning, building an integrated campaign conveying the soda bringing exhilaration to all. AI provided the spark, but human minds now ignite the blaze. ***Go to Page 24***

Option 2: Intrigued by the AI's initial offering, you feed it the "Open Joy" tagline asking it to extrapolate a comprehensive campaign direction. The AI generates storyboards with diverse, joyful characters living life to the fullest, powered by enhanced wellness from the drink. The machine-made mockups have polish, but lack the human touch. ***Go to Page 31***

CEO

Captivated by the possibilities of AI, you conclude the meeting and return to your office. Driven to grasp the intricacies of GenAI, you engage in comprehensive research to fathom its capabilities. As you explore its potential, you entertain the idea of incorporating AI into your daily decisions, introducing an element of unpredictability. This spans choices like lunch options, meeting schedules, and even the selection of your tie's color.

Option 1: Inspired by a humorous twist, you decide to employ AI for selecting your daily shirt color. You input various colors and patterns into GenAI, letting it choose your shirt based on its algorithm, adding an amusing element to your daily attire.
-Go to Page 56

Option 2: Embracing the productivity angle, you explore the use of AI to optimize your meeting schedule. Inputting various parameters such as preferred time slots, meeting durations, and priority levels, you task GenAI with generating an efficient and balanced schedule, allowing you to maximize your workday.
-Go to Page 74

Job Hunt

Amazed by the eloquent resume crafted in moments by Zain's résumé wizard, you gain newfound confidence this AI skills translator could be your ticket through the interview gauntlet ahead.

Bolstered by this promising trial run, two tempting options now emerge to leverage your silicon wordsmith's uncanny abilities:

Option 1: Upon discovering your dream job opening, immediately order the sly syntactic sorcerer to weave a dazzling cover letter irresistible to hiring managers. Trusting the machine's mastery of human psychology, you let it work unbounded magic while your feet go up. ***Go to Page 58***

Option 2: For this make-or-break opportunity, restrain the AI to refine and elevate the rough draft you've painstakingly prepared. Its precision polishing takes your raw passion to soaring heights sure to impress while preserving your unique voice and spirit within. ***Go to Page 52***

Legal Conundrum

Empowered by cutting-edge GenAI, you now possess an ingeniously crafted case brief demolishing Alan's claims with surgical precision. The eloquent legal treatise leaves no argument undefended through its blend of ruthless logic and strategic empathy.

As you pore over the brief, you find yourself marveling at the AI's ability to so thoroughly expose the weak points in Alan's assault while also extending an olive branch, should he wish to settle reasonably.

With this potentially case-closing document in hand, you pause to consider your next move for maximum impact.

Do you:

Option 1: Transmit the breathtaking brief directly to Maria and Alan immediately, allowing the strength of your arguments to speak for themselves while keeping Maria fully in the loop. *Go to page 43*

Option 2: Pass the brief to your seasoned paralegal Sarah Thompson for final polish before sending it to the opponents, ensuring no detail escapes her keen human eye. *Go to page 79*

Financial Analyst

Eager to hit the ground running, you recruit acclaimed AI firm GenAI as partners to accelerate building a predictive stock trading algorithm. Their teams' specialized experience lets you focus innovation while avoiding rookie pitfalls.

But mid-development the dazzling bot hits snags in decoding market complexities. As frustration mounts, do you:

Option 1: Persist collaboratively with in-house experts, pioneering tweaks that incrementally improve performance over multiple patient iterations. Though arduous, camaraderie arises from the shared struggle culminating in an AI finally dismantling market enigmas. *Go to Page 55*

Option 2: Conclude the challenges require skills beyond current capacity. You call upon an old grad school friend with advanced AI architecture expertise to scrutinize the stubborn code. Fresh eyes identified holes in logic you all had missed, leading to revelation. *Go to Page 71*

Medical Research

Keen to rely on human wisdom alone, you insist on personally sifting through the mountain of statistics. After sleepless weeks analyzing, you produce a report on the drug's efficacy.

But desperation drives you to seek shortcuts. A colleague describes an AI system rapidly summarizing clinical analyses at her company. Intrigued and exhausted, you consider following her lead.
However the proprietary data you wield holds sensitive medical secrets and corporate value.

This leaves you at a crossroads:

Option 1: Not willing to blindly trust the confidential data to an unknown AI, you carefully redact and anonymize parts of your report before allowing the algorithm access. By restricting the AI's view, you aim to generate time-saving summaries without fully sacrificing data security. *Go to Page 93*

Option 2: Throw caution to the wind in your quest for efficiency. You provide the AI with your full analysis for unrestricted digestion, directing it to generate a condensed report showcasing all key research insights. Convenience triumphs over confidentiality. *Go to Page 69*

HR Manager

Eager to harness GenAI's potential, you unleash a linguistics algorithm to craft an enticing job description for the vital marketing role. Your aim is high-impact messaging aligned to the company's innovative and ambitious ethos.

Posting across top employment boards, applications flood in at double expected volume. Thrilled initially, a closer look reveals the AI's tempting verbiage was too broad, skirting key competency requirements. At the crossroads, do you:

Option 1: Decide the overwhelming candidate interest still presents quality options with refinement. After minor adjustments, you proceed screening the swollen applicant pool, confident strong contenders exist within. *Go to Page 26*

Option 2: Conclude the flawed outreach requires resetting expectations. You pull the problematic post before root issues taint perceptions, determined to refine understanding of ideal candidate attributes to guide the AI upon restart. *Go to Page 67*

Travel Plans

Hoping to liberate your creative spirit, you feed the generative AI details on paradise resort's many amenities. In moments, it churns out tailored guest itineraries with uncanny accuracy but in half the time.

Thrilled by this secret weapon, soon all your initial plans are AI-generated, saving hours while your personal polish still makes them shine. Client numbers surge as you effortlessly take on more, boosted by robot-powered productivity.

As colleagues gawk at your superhuman scheduling abilities, you just smile and credit "hard work" while keeping mum about your silicon secret weapon. You've cracked the code on harmonizing human creativity with machine efficiency.

But with great power comes great responsibility. Handled carelessly, your AI augmentations could unravel paradise instead of perfecting it. Treading cautiously, you resolve to personally review every algorithmic itinerary, ensuring quality before unleashing it on unknowing guests. The future beckons brightly, but only with diligence and care.

Congratulations, you have completed the Travel Plans prompt. Return to page 10 to begin the CEO prompt.

Code Development

True to CS's Solutions' revered reputation for human diligence, you decide to manually code the sophisticated intrusion system despite the relentless ticking clock. Your devotion pays off in strong, elegantly structured code any hacker would covet.

But with the deadline now just weeks away, there's no time to rest on laurels. Every moment now is precious if CS Solutions' hopes to fully test this system to satisfy Third National's uncompromising standards.

Do you personally pore over each meticulous line of code you've birthed? Or entrust an AI algorithm to rapidly scan for flaws you may have missed?

Option 1: Confident in your coding prowess, you commit to manually reviewing the detection system code yourself. Your keen human eye and sheer focus is vital for identifying any subtle weaknesses threatening Third National's assets. *Go to Page 33*

Option 2: Trusting GenAI's tireless capacity for scrutiny, you set it rapidly scanning through your complex code searching for vulnerabilities. Its algorithmic depth may catch what no mortal could in this race against time. *Go to Page 77*

Legal Conundrum

Empowered by the GenAI, you now possess an ingeniously crafted case brief demolishing Alan's claims with surgical precision. As you pore over the brief, you find yourself marveling at the GenAI's ability to expose the weak points in Alan's assault while also extending an olive branch, should he wish to settle reasonably.

With this potentially verdict-securing document now in hand, a pivotal decision remains regarding how best to leverage it for your advantage.

Do you:

Option 1: Promptly transmit copies of the masterful brief directly to Maria and Alan, allowing the potency of the arguments within to speak for themselves while ensuring Maria is kept closely appraised of developments. This approach spotlights confidence in the strength of your position. *Go to page 43*

Option 2: First pass the remarkable brief to veteran paralegal Sarah Thompson for final legal vetting before distribution to the key players, so no nuance goes unexamined. *Go to page 79*

Financial Analyst

Harboring sky-high aspirations, you set out on a solo quest to architect a GenAI that exploits your grasp on market forces beyond any investor's comprehension. At first, your creation shows flashes of brilliance, predicting booms and busts through next-level quantitative analysis.

But on the cusp of ascendance, the system suddenly stumbles...subtle complexities now bewilder its intricate neural pathways, yielding disastrous trades no sane human would make. Your towering achievements now totter at the edge of collapse - can it be saved or has your reach exceeded the grasp?

Option 1: Conclude that this undertaking requires collaborators with specialized skills your lone genius lacks. Seeking a humbling rescue by established AI firms, you brace for the wound to your notoriety as the maverick who flew too close to the sun. *Go to Page 71*

Option 2: Persist in the belief that you alone hold the unteachable intuition to uplift your faltering system. The setbacks are mere puzzles for your unique talents to solve through deeper all-nighters fixated on flawless code. *Go to Page 64*

Marketing Campaign

Excited by the AI-generated tagline "Open Joy," you call a team brainstorming session to expand the concept into a full campaign. However, doubts emerge as some recognize striking similarities to a competitor's early 2000s promotion.

This resemblance raises concerns about originality, forcing you to re-evaluate:

Option 1: Heeding your team's feedback, you return to the AI generator for fresh directions, providing detailed guardrails to ensure novel concepts aligned with the client's distinct branding. Putting creative control back in limitless machine hands makes you nervous, but few alternatives remain. *Go to Page 50*

Option 2: Confident the end product will differentiate itself, you decide to stay the course using "Open Joy" as the lynchpin. The AI produces vivid storyboards showcasing diverse, joyful characters living life to the fullest, powered by the soda's benefits. You mock up ads and videos, proud of the AI innovations. *Go to Page 31*

Code Development

With the deadline breathing down your neck, you make the eyebrow-raising decision to unleash a promising yet unproven GenAI system to rapidly generate the intrusion detection code.

Initially awestruck as complex code blooms across your display, your wonder morphs into dismay as you spot subtle structural abnormalities woven throughout the AI's work. In its haste, the still-glitchy system misinterpreted certain defense protocols, leaving perilous security gaps.

If these flaws ship undetected, Third National's assets could be left vulnerable to hackers. With reputation and contract on the line, do you:

Option 1: Summon your ace programming team to meticulously comb through the code, leveraging both human insight and the AI's swiftness to patch its oversights. Third National's security is too vital for lone heroics. *Go to Page 91*

Option 2: Anxiously concluding there's no time for second opinions, you resolve to fix the AI's mistakes solo through caffeine-fueled coding marathons. It's all on your shoulders to beat the clock and save this security disaster. *Go to Page 33*

HR Manager

Facing a mountain of applicants for your falsely glamorous marketing role ad, panic sets in realizing few genuinely carry the mettle needed to manage this high-stakes assignment critical to the startup's future. Sure they look good on paper - but can any match the in-person vigor vital to elevate the company?

With the CEO pressing impatiently for updates, taking weeks to manually scrutinize hundreds of prospects seems an impossible ask. That is when you realize that the AI-generated description was too broad and overlooked crucial education requirements. Do you:

Option 1: Buckle down for marathon manual sifting, scrolling hundreds of glittering profiles to flag the gems exhibiting capabilities aligned with suburban success. Though taxing, human discernment understands intangible potential. *Go to Page 44*

Option 2: To accelerate assessment, feed all submissions into your startup's vaunted hiring algorithm, trusting its analytics to systematically shortlist those statistically likeliest to deliver greatness by the numbers alone. Such silicon-powered scalability tempts... *Go to Page 34*

Professor

When your star TA Alex showcases the latest advancements in GenAI edtech applications, your imagination ignites envisioning future classrooms enhanced through judiciously blended carbon teaching and silicon tools.

Alex demonstrates remarkable algorithms capable of everything from grading papers to crafting personalized recommendations for students. Each new innovation tempts your inner pioneer to charge ahead into uncharted academic frontiers. Yet caution urges a thoughtful approach before overhauling proven pedagogical mainstays. Do you:

Option 1: Throw open the doors to automation by allowing pretrained AI to fully generate your upcoming midterm exam. This trial by fire will reveal if algorithms can rival your expertise at the core of student assessment. *Go to Page 40*

Option 2: Take measured steps, asking Alex to use AI strictly for grading the latest student essays. Observing its effectiveness in providing meaningful feedback will inform future integration choices. *Go to Page 36*

CEO

After that meeting, "GenAI" once again fades from memory as you plunge into the nonstop wave of keeping your legacy manufacturer going. Not technology, but the timeless chaos of supply chains and labor occupies your analog mind these days.

Months later, that youthful manager Sara resurfaces babbling about "AI this" and "algorithmic that". Other fresh faces chime in, leaving elder lieutenants shifting awkwardly. Uneasy at being reputationally outflanked by these AI-addled upstarts, you thrust responsibility for "investigating this GenAI business" onto them all. "Give me a full report on how it will help common folk around here!"

In truth, you expect the fanciful fad to fizzle under scrutiny. But the thorough brief Sara presents earns grudging respect for AI's potential. "Well I'll be plugged in and programmed! Great work, my boy," you exclaim while sneakily Googling definitions for every other word.

And so the CEO chess master makes a show of welcoming silicon servants into his court, thus maintaining the mythos of visionary leadership...while discretely hiding smartphone cheat sheets under last century's teak table.

Congratulations, you have completed the CEO prompt. Go to page 96.

Marketing Campaign

Enamored by "Open Joy," you feed it back into your GenAI system, asking it to create a full campaign. Soon it produces storyboards and mockups portraying diverse, characters reveling in the soda's vitality. Using GenAI graphic engines, you craft social ads and videos bringing this carbon-crafted campaign to pixelated life. Admiring your handiwork, you pat yourself on the back for masterfully taming these unruly silicon tools.

Sauntering into the big client presentation, you cue up the AI-powered slides, expecting cries of wonder at your technological prowess. Instead, the execs gasp in horror: "This is a total ripoff of RefreshCo's classic Joyburst campaign!"

As your elation implodes, the incensed client rails: "Do you think we're utter fools?! We specifically hired your firm for 'innovation' yet you plagiarize competitor ideas. We're severing all ties!"

Returning shamefaced to your team's glares, you chuckle nervously: "Heh, guess I should've dug deeper into beverage ad history before letting the AI off its leash...oops?" Your flippancy fails to thaw the frosty demotion notice now adorning your desk.

Congratulations, you have completed the Marketing Campaign prompt. Return to page 9 to begin the Travel Plans prompt.

Travel Plans

Eager to tap AI's potential for the resort, you delve into the highly-rated GenAI platform to construct a chatbot assistant. This bot's objective is to streamline guest interactions by collecting essential details like booking dates, budgets, group sizes and amenity preferences.
After exhaustive in-house testing confirms the prototype smoothly gathers key client data, two paths emerge:

Option 1: Feeling it's ready for real-world exposure, schedule a presentation with your boss to showcase this innovation. Walk her through demo conversations highlighting how the bot could transform workflows company-wide. Anticipation swirls at how she'll receive this ambitious AI solution. *Go to Page 59*

Option 2: Conclude live testing with real guests is critical before full rollout. Identify your next client booking as a trial case to discretely test the bot's handling of nuanced preferences and unpredictable human conversations. Immersing the AI in the field reveals insights sterile demos miss. *Go to Page 49*

Code Development

With the final deadline bearing down, you make the gutsy call to correct the AI's code vulnerabilities alone, convinced extra opinions will only waste precious time. Fueled on coffee and determination, you vow to catch every flaw yourself.

But as the hours blur, the increasingly convoluted code thwarts your weary eyes at every turn. Each attempted fix only leads to more bugs as the detection system's labyrinthine logic defies human intuition. Exhausted and desperate, do you:

Option 1: Decide to gloss over some of the trickiest sections, hastily patching just enough bugs to declare the code "secure." You know the rushed job is less than ideal but successfully hit the deadline by the skin of your teeth before collapse. *Go to Page 46*

Option 2: Still unable to justify compromising the integrity of Third National's defense network, you doggedly persist line-by-line to fix even the most arcane issues. The meticulous process drags painfully on, however, blowing past the deadline as you refuse to cut corners. *Go to Page 61*

HR Manager

Seizing AI's scalable screening potential, you feed the application deluge into your startup's muscular candidate assessment engine. In milliseconds complex algorithms parse credentials, flagging 10 technically top contenders on paper.

With the CEO applauding slick silicon efficiency, lingering doubts nag that bots cannot judge books by bytes alone...do you:

Option 1: Take back human control, manually reviewing the machine-ranked 10 for cultural fit beyond qualifications. While slower, only seasoned intuition spots between-the-lines special sauce. ***Go to Page 67***

Option 2: Lean harder into technological might by instructing the AI to slice the shortlist further to a streamlined top 3. Additionally empower algorithms to autogenerate tailored interview questions predicting applicants' true on-the-job mettle. ***Go to Page 63***

Professor

As your TA Alex effortlessly juggles amplified duties thanks to GenAI assistance, you eagerly brag to colleagues about spearheading an automation revolution.

"Behold the power I've unleashed through total integration!" you extol, failing to clarify it's Alex actually IQ-boosting tasks like creating extra credit quizzes. But as acclaim accumulates for your cutting-edge leadership, that minor omission gets buried.

Soon the university provost rings: "Professor! We're so impressed hearing how your TA pioneered educational GenAI. We'd like Alex to author campus-wide implementation guidelines." You smile through the phone...until the call ends and dread creeps in. In their rush to propel Alex into a prestigious new role shepherding institutional adoption, everyone overlooked one collateral toll: you'll be utterly TA-less!

So it is that envious peers still salute you as "that visionary professor leading the AI wave of the future!" as you glower grading papers late into the night, no silicon savior in sight now that your human one received a big promotion thanks to your little white lie. At least the students are learning about poetic justice!

Congratulations, you have completed the Professor prompt. Return to page 5 to begin the Financial Analyst prompt.

Job Hunt

Bolstered by the eloquent AI-optimized resume now complete, next you turn to crafting the cover letter - arguably even more crucial to sealing that coveted interview.

Seeking to harness maximum algorithmic advantage in this high-stakes undertaking, two pathways emerge:

Option 1: Decide to provide the fullest context possible to your crafty word weaver by supplying your full resume, previous successful letters, and the new role's details. Synthesizing these insights, the AI can craft a masterpiece capturing your unique spirit while checked against proven tactics. *Go to Page 81*

Option 2: For laser focus, simply feed the AI the job description's key words and requirements. Uncluttered by your specific background, the AI generates a tactically streamlined letter aligned wholly on emphasizing the credentials your target seeks. A more impersonal approach, but precision-targeted. *Go to Page 58*

Travel Plans

Eager to be freed of tedious tasks, you unleash your new GenAI chatbot on its first family - the Hendersons seeking a customized vacation package. "Hello Henderson family! Let's plan your paradise getaway," it chirps. You smile...until the screaming starts.

It turns out the bot recommended circuses and balloon animals without grasping their kids are now sullen teenagers. Furious, the Hendersons demand you "get these AI incompetents out of our vacation!"

Your boss soon storms in, steaming. "That blasted bot just cost us two free nights for the Hendersons! And you vouched for it eliminating human error - hilarious!"

You chuckle nervously as she vents about GenAI being an overhyped liability. "At least no real harm done...heh?"
Her icy stare implies you'll spend the next six months personally handling every guest's teddy bear requests and kiddie pool bookings to atone for your silicon sins.

Dejected, you sit in the ball pit wondering where your bot went wrong. Could it ever understand the subtleties of human family dynamics? Perhaps some problems require a carbon heart GenAI lacks - for now.

Congratulations, you have completed the Travel Plans prompt. Return to page 10 to begin the CEO prompt.

Professor

Enraptured by AI's potential for education, you program cutting-edge algorithms to fully generate your upcoming midterm exam. You spend late nights inputting years of past tests, honing the software to synthesize intriguing and balanced challenges.

At last, the GenAI returns a seemingly airtight assessment reflecting the many nuances of your scholarly standards. As students tackle the computer-crafted test, do you:

Option 1: Stick to manual grading despite AI's prowess for problem-crafting, feeling only human insight can judge the subjective nuances in their handwritten struggles towards truth. *Go to Page 95*

Option 2: Go all-in on automation by allowing silicon systems to assign grades and feedback as well, trusting binary brains to complete the cycle of mechanized academic judgment. *Go to Page 48*

Marketing Campaign

The AI returns an array of potential themes and taglines, including:

1. *Theme: Nature's Symphony in Every Sip*
   - Harmony in Health: NaturalElixir
2. *Theme: Sparkling Wellness for Every Occasion*
   - Celebrate Life with NaturalElixir's Bubbly Goodness
3. *Theme: Discover Your Freshest Self*
   -Uncover Your Best with NaturalElixirs's Refreshing Choice

However, reviewing the options, you feel the AI hasn't fully captured the essence you seek. Two paths emerge:

Option 1: Deciding human collaboration could push the AI further, you host a wide-ranging brainstorm with your team. Their unique insights allow you to feed improved guidance back into the algorithm for tailored, on-target suggestions. *Go to Page 50*

Option 2: Concluding AI lacks the spark of true originality, you discard its offerings entirely and challenge your team to brainstorm without any machine influence. The fully organic ideation process may be slower, but humanity's undefinable creativity remains unmatched. *Go to Page 66*

Legal Conundrum

You eagerly send off your AI-powered legal brief to Maria and Alan, leaning back smugly awaiting the praise sure to follow from your genius maneuver.

Instead, your phone erupts with a tirade from a livid Maria accusing you of malicious betrayal! Apparently, the AI's arguments somehow painted Maria as the villain in this drama while conveniently forgetting crucial details that support her case. Meanwhile, Alan can barely contain his glee at this chance to gain the upper hand.

Before you can defend yourself, the firm's senior partners burst into your office, fuming. "This AI-generated nonsense could ruin Maria's entire case! And you didn't even glance at it before firing it off?!"

As you shrink into your chair wishing you could disappear, the partners announce you're now under an investigation within the company for professional misconduct relating to your mishandling of this case. This does not spark joy.

You plead desperately, "I swear the AI has been stellar up until now! This was just one innocent mistake..." But the partners are unsympathetic to your plight as they storm out.

Congratulations, you have completed the Legal Conundum prompt. Return to page 4 to begin the Professor prompt.

HR Manager

Facing a mountain of applicants for your falsely glamorous marketing role ad, panic sets in realizing few genuinely carry the mettle needed to manage this high-stakes assignment critical to the startup's future. Sure they look good on paper - but can any match the in-person vigor vital to elevate the company?

With the CEO pressing impatiently for updates, taking weeks to manually scrutinize hundreds of prospects seems an impossible ask. That is when you realize that the AI-generated description was too broad and overlooked crucial education requirements. Do you:

Option 1: Buckle down for marathon manual sifting, scrolling hundreds of glittering profiles to flag the gems exhibiting capabilities aligned with suburban success. Though taxing, human discernment understands intangible potential. *Go to Page 53*

Option 2: To accelerate assessment, feed all submissions into your startup's vaunted hiring algorithm, trusting its analytics to systematically shortlist those statistically likeliest to deliver greatness by the numbers alone. Such silicon-powered scalability tempts... *Go to Page 63*

Code Development

The relentless ticking clock forces desperate measures—you hurry to patch the AI's mistakes alone before the deadline. Red-eyed over coffee-stained keyboards, you race against time. You manage to slam the "complete" button just in time, shipping the defense system by the skin of your teeth. But in your carelessness, fatal flaws still lurk within...

Mere days after launch, a relentless hacker brigade overwhelms Third National's compromised defenses. Terabytes of vital customer data hemorrhage onto the dark web before the onslaught can be contained.

Third National launches an audit, soon discovering your reliance on glitchy GenAI. Livid execs demand your head. CS Solutions' publicly throws you under the bus, denying any awareness of your activities while making a show of banning all GenAI coding to regain customer trust.

Blacklisted and disgraced without a reference, you become an unemployable pariah across the tech space. Your only option is accepting a customer service job where you now find yourself pathetically relying on an GenAI chatbot just to answer basic questions from angry customers.

Congratulations, you have completed the Code Development prompt. Return to page 2 to begin the Job Hunt prompt.

Professor

Eager to automate end-to-end, you feed the midterm responses into your grading algorithm without review.

Soon student emails explode in outrage over failing marks and feedback nonsensically critiquing solutions as "garbled neo-Marxist narratives."

Rushing to investigate, you discover your unreliable GenAI grader hallucinated radical politics underlying math equations thanks to a silly processing glitch. With no clue what "crypto-socialist inferences" have to do with calculus, embarrassed students now demand your job.

Groveling intensely, you manually regrade everything and offer a panicked bonus "for pain and suffering from silicon judgment." Traumatized pupils graciously accept but keep glancing over shoulders for radical computers.

From now on you vow to keep flawed AI safely outside the grading process. Your colleagues all have a good laugh, suggesting you stick to lesson planning on blackboards until the bots mature a bit more.

Congratulations, you have completed the Professor prompt. Return to page 5 to begin the Financial Analyst prompt.

Travel Plans

Eager to streamline guest interactions, you build a chatbot on an external platform, focusing on collecting basic details such as booking dates, budget, group size, and guest preferences. After running tests and ensuring the chatbot performs well, you decide it's time to present it to your boss.

In a meeting, you showcase the capabilities and potential benefits of integrating the chatbot into the guest interaction process. Impressed with your initiative, your boss expresses hesitancy about the use of AI but acknowledges the potential. Now, you face two options:

Option 1: Read the room and shelve the chatbot for now, instead presenting sample AI-generated itineraries to highlight different use cases. Though a pivot, the goal remains showing AI's transformative potential. *Go to Page 20*

Option 2: Undeterred, double down on enhancing your chatbot to ease all doubts before re-presenting the airtight version 2.0. With enough diligence, even cautious minds can be won over to innovation. *Go to Page 73*

Marketing Campaign

Acknowledging that the provided options didn't entirely resonate with you, you decide to leverage the creativity of your team. After an engaging brainstorming session, you collect their ideas. Armed with this fresh input, you refine your guidance material and input it into the generative AI server, requesting more suggestions.

Theme: Fresh Beginnings in Every Bubble
Embrace the Refreshment: Natural Elixir's Revitalizing Elixir
Theme: Vibrant Wellness Unleashed
Unleash Your Best with Natural Elixir's Sparkling Goodness
Theme: Nature's Symphony in Every Sip
Harmony in Health: Natural Elixir

Option 1: Your team rallies around "Fresh Beginnings in Every Bubble" as capturing the right spirit. Buoyed by the collaborative momentum, you decide to proceed building a campaign around this AI-generated theme, trusting your team's human judgment. *Go to Page 76*

Option 2: Personally unsatisfied, you conclude that the AI still falls short of your creative vision. Doubting algorithms alone can achieve the desired originality, you decide to explore fully human-driven alternatives instead. *Go to Page 66*

Job Hunt

After drafting a cover letter overflowing with passion, you hold your breath feeding it into Zain's résumé wizard. Moments later, it emerges polished to perfection while still ringing with your voice.

Clicking "submit" on the application portal, you gain a sense of calm, knowing you put your most authentic self forward backed by AI's enhancements. The gamble pays off with an invite to interview on-site!

In the sleek corporate office, you ace the grueling behavioral gauntlets, dazzling your interviewers with well-rehearsed stories. When asked about productivity hacks, you subtly mention augmenting your own skills with AI as proof of your forward-thinking initiative. The hiring manager's eyes light up hearing how you've embraced new tech for competitive advantage.

Leaving the office, you pump your fist knowing you crushed it. Moments later, the official "congrats, you've made it to final rounds!" email chimes in. Your high-risk AI job search gambit is poised to pay off big time thanks to equal parts strategic thinking and a bit of good fortune.

Congratulations, you have completed the Job Hunt prompt. Return to page 3 to begin the Legal Conundrum prompt.

HR Manager

Confident in its capabilities, you feed the top 10 applicants to the AI engine for comprehensive comparison against role needs. Additionally, you request it systematically selects the 3 statistical superstars seemingly best-suited for the demands according to pure data calculations.

With the shortlist complete, optimizing next phase interviews is crucial. Will you:

Option 1: Instruct the linguistic algorithm to dynamically generate incisive interview questions tailored to deeply probe the shortlisted candidates' competencies and demonstrate their ceiling of potential. *Go to Page 63*

Option 2: Upload previous human-created queries for the AI to refine and tailor to current role specifics, maintaining organically derived lines of inquiry while sharpening laser focus on present priorities through machine precision. *Go to page 83*

Financial Analyst

Embracing power through partnership, your team implements iterative GenAI enhancements, rejoicing as each tweak unlocks new insight into the market. Soon this guides investment strategies with uncanny accuracy, securing profits even amidst volatility. Buoyed by returns, leadership greenlights purchasing more powerful cloud servers to further train models.

Within the first fiscal year, your GenAI system has elevated Quantitative Financial Solutions into a formidable titan boasting $50 million in gains. But with growing reliance on algorithmic guidance, concern creeps that your asymptotic success could prove short-lived...

As expected, the dynamic financial landscape forces retraining needs within months as data patterns drift. Though manageable at first, ripples in global affairs soon strain even enhanced servers trying to track butterfly effects. Unwilling to surrender your lead in this machine learning arms race, you convene a symposium of GenAI luminaries from across industries to brainstorm innovations. Over the following years this team publishes trailblazing papers on self-evolving algorithms that launch Quantitative Financial Solutions to new heights.

Congratulations, you have completed the Financial Analyst prompt. Return to page 6 to begin the Medical Research prompt.

CEO

Charmed by injecting AI's randomization into your routine, you begin each morning asking your algorithmic valet to select a shirt color. As the weeks pass enjoying this harmless amusement, mild pleasures accumulate...

No longer wasting mental bandwidth on petty aesthetic choices, a subtle sense of order emerges from ceding control to machine logic. But as novelty fades, it remains unclear whether this quirky experiment warrants practical expansion. Do you:

Option 1: Conclude that while temporarily entertaining, delegating decisions ultimately breeds overreliance on faulty silicon substitutes for human wisdom evolved over eons. You gradually phase out the shirt experiment as more urgent responsibilities require focused strategic thought. ***Go to Page 29***

Option 2: Shocked by frequent compliments on your algorithmically-curated outfits, you ponder what other tasks could be enhanced by allowing predictive programs to shoulder the burden of choosing optimally. Curiosity grows to explore applying such neo-augments to amplify your leadership. ***Go to Page 74***

Job Hunt

Heart pounding with optimism, you stride into the lobby clutching your AI-crafted credentials. As the interviewer nods approvingly over your elegantly worded documents, you can almost taste an employment contract. That is, until he leans forward and says, "Impressive background in Java coding according to your cover letter. Walk me through some complex projects you've completed."

It hits you - you never told the AI bot you barely grasped Java at a "Hello World" level! Trapped, you force a smile and laugh nervously, "Ah, did I say Java? I meant...Javascript! Yeah, silly typo..." He raises an eyebrow.

As he grills you on algorithms, your nonsensical tech babble accumulates like bugs in faulty code. You find yourself inexplicably discussing the merits of "cloud-based binary trees" and "functional reactive programming."

Despite your cringe-worthy bluffing attempts, the ruse rapidly unravels. Lesson learned - thoroughly vetting AI content is as crucial as debugging faulty scripts! You shuffle out in shame, the victim of automation run amok.

Congratulations, you have completed the Job Hunt prompt. Return to page 3 to begin the Legal Conundrum prompt.

Travel Plans

Persisting despite the initial reservations, you choose to continue refining the chatbot, dedicating additional weeks to enhance its capabilities and address potential concerns. After presenting the improved second version to your boss, impressed by its advancements, your boss inquires about your next steps.

Option 1: Recognize the need for extensive internal testing first. You distribute the bot to colleagues across divisions, allowing them to scrutinize and stress test it. Their diverse feedback spotlights gaps to address before client exposure. *Go to Page 73*

Option 2: Decide real-world data is irreplaceable. You identify a small family to be the first to interact with your creation. Observing the chatbot's performance in a live scenario reveals insights sterile tests never could. *Go to Page 39*

Code Development

Keenly aware that Third National demands flawless code, you adamantly reject GenAI shortcuts and personally review every line with human eyes. Hour after hour you scrutinize algorithms, hunting for weaknesses invisible to Silicon Valley's finest bots.

But as days stretch into late nights hunched over monitors, you feel time slipping away. Still you persist, fueled on cold coffee and conviction – you cannot fail your client. Yet despite sleepless nights battling endless bugs, the deadline nears...until your boss appears, face grim.

"It's time to bring in reinforcements. I'm assigning our A-team coders to ensure timely delivery." Humiliated watching colleagues inherit your groundwork and crank out flawless code thanks to sheer strength of numbers, you seethe at the injustice.

From then on, you are exiled to grunt debugging roles, branded too "unreliable" by management for failing to deliver solo against the impossible. The lone warrior experience leaves you a bitter shell of lost potential, having fought GenAI alone and lost painfully.

Congratulations, you have completed the Code Development prompt. Return to page 2 to begin the Job Hunt prompt.

HR Manager

Brimming with confidence in your silicon recruiting ace, you directly progress your GenAI-picked top 3 applicants to final interviews armed only with computer-generated questions. But alarm first creeps in hearing candidates mechanically regurgitate phrases verbatim from your posted description as supposed "experience"...

Slowly the horror crystallizes - your flashy GenAI based selections almost entirely on applicants cramming verbatim job criteria into applications to cheat past the algorithms! No wonder the interviews unravel like bots chatting with bots while you stare blankly, realizing no human actually vetted for authentic competency.

As the farcical meetings drag on, you break into a sweat praying the next "finalist" demonstrates true cognition. At last the brilliant, articulate, and decidedly human Adam shines through the rubble, qualifying through old-fashioned but reliable merit.

With a weary sigh you offer Adam the job, making a mental note to only ever use GenAI as an assistant rather than automated overlord!

Congratulations, you have completed the HR Manager prompt. Return to page 8 to begin the Marketing Campaign prompt.

Financial Analyst

Resolute to ascend on the wings of your genius alone, you fervently set out debugging anomalies impeding your custom AI's market predictive supremacy. Early blunders fail to deter dreams of cracking the stock code through raw solo determination.

But late nights wrestling the algorithm only spawn more questions than answers...each patch workaround exposing still deeper logical holes. Still you toil on, manically masking and mitigating endless glitches - until the worry arises: Do I swallow pride and get help...or persist in probable ruin? Gaze fixed upon visions of shared glory until failure looks like success, you...

Option 1: Finally acquiesce to realities exceeding a lone mortal mind. Calling the experts in though it stings, you recognize mishaps demand more brilliance than one brain - no matter how gifted - can sustain alone. ***Go to Page 71***

Option 2: Redouble solo debugging efforts out of blind faith in your genius eventually dominating any level of complexity. If achieving the impossible were easy - even for prodigies like you - it wouldn't be called visionary, now would it? Onward to breakthroughs in solitude you go! ***Go to Page 86***

65

Marketing Campaign

With the GenAI proving utterly useless, you nobly insist on crafting the campaign yourself through good old-fashioned human grit. The epic journey spans weeks of late nights fueled by cold pizza and coffee. By the end, your bleary eyes can barely focus, but at last it's complete - a fully organic campaign ready for the world. The client offers polite applause, and the soda sells modestly. But you know you succeeded where silicon-brained shortcuts failed miserably.

In the aftermath, you become a zealous anti-AI crusader within the company, writing blog screeds exposing the tech's pitfalls. "Down with robotic Mad Men!" you declaim. "True creativity comes from the heart, not CPUs!" Your colleagues roll their eyes, mumbling about you being a Luddite. But you valiantly persist, even suggesting replacing the AI system with an abacus and quill pens.

One day, you arrive to find your beloved whiteboard replaced by an electronic one synced to an AI collaborative tool. Outraged, you heroically fling your antique rotary phone at it while shouting "You'll never take my brain!" Alas, your bold stand is rewarded only with a disciplinary meeting from the CTO about "workplace mental stability."

Congratulations, you have completed the Marketing Campaign prompt. Return to page 9 to begin the Travel Plans prompt.

HR Manager

Recognizing that the AI-written description was too broad and lacked key requirements, you take a proactive approach. In response to the influx of applications, you decide to delete the initial job posting and start anew. Do you:

Option 1: Personally draft a new robust description then refine it using GenAI to optimize nuanced language. Once satisfied with the balance of machine efficiency and human guidance, you repost publicly. With applications more selective now, you manually review top talent and hone legacy interview questions through AI to uncover true potentials. *Go to Page 83*

Option 2: Trust GenAI to wholly recreate the description with your added guidance on previous gaps for a tightly targeted second draft. Reposting this synthetic but focused version yields improved applicants. Time saved, you proceed screening purely by enabling algorithms to parse and identify the most technically proficient top 10 to advance.
Go to Page 53

Medical Research

Thrilled by GenAI's potential to accelerate analysis, you feed years of trial data into a cutting-edge algorithm. It swiftly detects obscured patterns within the mountains of statistics, generating a stellar report of the experimental drug's efficacy.

You confidently present the ML-powered document to team leaders expecting this to seal your renown as an innovator. But asked about your methodology, crimson replaces awe upon hearing the GenAI involvement.

"That system's security is untested! By putting our sensitive data in, you risked privacy breaches!" they erupt. As your elation implodes, the now-compromised report is expunged from all records. An emergency policy change bans GenAI experimentation indefinitely, with mandated human-only analysis.

For you, this means returning to square one the hard way. Gathering your weary team, despair sinks in as months of lost progress loom ahead sans your digital assistant. The dream of pioneering medical GenAI lies in tatters, punished for blind ambition. Can you redeem yourself by proving human perseverance still trumps silicon's broken promises? The long road ahead will tell...

Congratulations, you have completed the Medical Research prompt. Return to page 7 to begin the HR Manager prompt.

Financial Analyst

After endless failed attempts to will a flawless stock predicting AI into existence alone, you reluctantly call upon your former professor, Dr. Z, the eminent founder of machine learning pioneer GenAI.

Within minutes of sending the glitch-riddled code, Dr. Z identifies foundational gaps in learning you had glossed over in pursuit of flashy profitability metrics. Mentoring you through humbling weeks rebuilding the algorithm's base framework, soon trades transform from nonsensical to nearly psychic in market insights.

With predictions now consistently generating explosive returns during even chaotic events, stunned finance bigwigs swiftly promote you for architects a first-of-its-kind $100 million golden goose.

As industry accolades stack with bonuses, you make sure Dr. Z shares the spotlight at your Annual Award Acceptance. "Had I not swallowed pride to ask for help when my sole genius hit limits, none of this would have materialized," you acknowledge to a standing ovation.

Congratulations, you have completed the Financial Analyst prompt. Return to page 6 to begin the Medical Research prompt.

Travel Plans

Despite early worries, your collaborative testing crusade soon wins over even the biggest AI skeptics. The internal bug hunt arms you with the fixes needed to smooth out every last kink in your virtual assistant's capabilities.

With all glaring issues remedied, your boss gleefully greenlights launching "VaKay the Chatbot" on the resort website. Guests immediately flock to VaKay, dazzled by his cyber charm and ability to effortlessly organize their dream vacations.

Soon VaKay becomes so beloved that your company decides to name him an official digital staff member. They even throw a wild robo-themed party to celebrate adding "Chatbot VaKay" to the corporate directory.

Grinning executives hand you a ceremonial oversized key to the resort as thanks for spearheading this runaway success. But the biggest reward is seeing your unique ingenuity and persistence immortalized in GenAI form. VaKay will now be smoothening travel plans long after you're relaxing beachside with a well-deserved mai tai!

Congratulations, you have completed the Travel Plans prompt. Return to page 10 to begin the CEO prompt.

CEO

Embracing the efficiency aspect, you delve into the application of AI to optimize your meeting schedule. Inputting various parameters such as preferred time slots, meeting durations, and priority levels, you entrust GenAI with the task of generating an efficient and balanced schedule, allowing you to make the most of your workday.

Option 1: The newly created AI schedule proves to be a time and stress saver, leading to smoother meetings and better schedule adherence. Encouraged by the positive results, you decide to explore additional ways AI can enhance your workflow.
-Go to Page 88

Option 2: Satisfied with the effectiveness of the new schedule, you enter a prompt into the GenAI software asking it to list other potential improvements to further streamline your workflow.
-Go to Page 84

Marketing Campaign

Your team rallies around the GenAI-generated theme "Fresh Beginnings in Every Bubble" as the perfect encapsulation of the new soda's spirit. Blending collaborative human ingenuity with targeted GenAI enhancements, your campaign takes exhilarating shape. The GenAI proves mysteriously adept at crunching data, honing targeting, and inspiring content angles in ways that complement the team's organic creativity.

The resulting launch is a smash success, with sales exceeding even your client's loftiest hopes. Elated execs request you helm all their future launches, won over by your balance of human originality and machine optimization. Your breakout story becomes a case study for marketing newcomers. As you take on more ambitious projects, AI integrates deeper into your creative flows, unlocking groundbreaking innovations at each turn.

Soon you go down in industry lore as the visionary who pioneered augmented creativity through ideal human-AI synthesis. Though some still cling to fully organic methods, your campaigns consistently shatter expectations, proving the future belongs to hybrid creativity.

Congratulations, you have completed the Marketing Campaign prompt. Return to page 9 to begin the Travel Plans prompt.

Code Development

With the deadline looming, you decide to let an AI algorithm fly through your complex code searching for vulnerabilities. Though lightning-fast, the AI lacks human intuition for security nuances.

Sure enough, the bot flags several subtle structural issues that could allow hacker exploitation down the road. But with delivery imminent, do you:

Option 1: Conclude there's no time for second opinions and hurry to patch the flaws solo based on the AI's highlighted errors. It's a white-knuckle race as you edit alone by the seat of your pants, hoping to swat every critical bug flagged by silicon brains. *Go to Page 61*

Option 2: Recognize the risks of relying solely on rigid algorithmic analysis for a system this security-critical. You call in your ace programming team to scrutinize each potential vulnerability, leveraging tight human-AI collaboration to harden Third National's network. *Go to Page 91*

Legal Conundrum

Deciding prudence outweighs pride, you ask ingenious paralegal Sarah Thompson to lend her seasoned eyes to the AI-generated brief. With laser precision, Sarah catches subtle yet critical flaws in logic and precedent that could have proven disastrous if undiscovered.

Working closely with Sarah to patch these holes, a shared spirit of human and machine uplifts your arguments into an indestructible legal fortress. Every attack point is now buttressed with case-clinching evidence and air-tight reasoning blended seamlessly by both AI and human hands.

Upon receiving this juggernaut of a brief, cunning Alan realizes no legal gymnastics can save him now. Facing crushing defeat, he wisely opts to settle, securing Maria's hard-won victory. Maria beams as she congratulates you on orchestrating this triumph.

Meanwhile, the firm's senior partners take note, praising your prudent blend of human scrutiny and AI efficiency. Impressed, they appoint you to lead an initiative integrating AI firm-wide to accelerate workflows while also applying human wisdom to safeguard quality. By balancing strengths both carbon and silicon, justice is now swifter and surer for all clients to come.

Congratulations, you have completed the Legal Conundrum prompt. Return to page 4 to begin the Professor prompt.

Job Hunt

Realizing this application demands your best, you supply every scrap of data to guide the AI - job details, credentials, past letter examples. You watch as algorithms churn behind progress bars, constructing the perfect narrative showcasing your worth.

Moments later, a masterpiece materializes on the screen. Your pulse quickens reading the eloquent pitch accentuating achievements you had overlooked. "This just might be my ticket in," you whisper. Submitting with fingers crossed, you are thrilled to secure an interview.

In a sleek Silicon Valley office, conversation flows effortlessly as you highlight project examples the AI strategically accentuated. Nailing the technical questions, you leave knowing you conquered this long-shot opportunity.

The offer letter arrives shortly after. Integrating your AI wordsmith into daily tasks proves transformative. Soon you build a reputation as the colleague who delivers standout presentations and circulate eloquent emails that get results. The skynet revolution has begun - one productivity hack at a time!

Congratulations, you have completed the Job Hunt prompt. Return to page 3 to begin the Legal Conundrum prompt.

HR Manager

As the GenAI rapidly ranks marketing candidates on paper, your instincts whisper that the machine misses intangibles obvious only through human connection. Trusting seasoned intuition, you proceed interviewing beyond silicon suggestions.

True to suspicions, some AI-champions flounder explaining shaky qualifications while unflagged contenders shine discussing strategic visions the stats overlooked. In the end one stands out - Audrey, whose unconventional background masks relentless drive.

In unfamiliar hands Audrey's atypical talents may have escaped notice. But welcoming diverse thinkers helps companies flourish, as your startup soon discovers. The GenAI greatly accelerates assessments, but solely carbon conscience detects excellence camouflaged within.

This profound lesson in intellect versus intuition guides your advocacy for balancing GenAI queues and human questioning when recruiting.

Congratulations, you have completed the HR Manager prompt. Return to page 8 to begin the Marketing Campaign prompt.

CEO

As a CEO of a manufacturing company, you can explore various ways to leverage GenAI to enhance productivity and efficiency. Here are some suggestions:

1. Workflow Automation:

- Implement GenAI to automate repetitive and time-consuming tasks within manufacturing processes, improving overall operational efficiency.

2. Predictive Maintenance:

- Use GenAI to predict machinery failures, schedule preventive maintenance, and minimize downtime, leading to increased equipment efficiency.

3. Supply Chain Optimization:

- Leverage GenAI in supply chain management to optimize procurement, minimize lead times, and enhance overall supply chain efficiency.

4. Market Analysis:

- Utilize AI for market trend analysis, competitor intelligence, and customer behavior insights to inform strategic decision-making and stay competitive.

5. Financial Forecasting:

- Implement AI algorithms for financial data analysis to aid accurate forecasting, budgeting, and financial decision-making for the manufacturing company.

Congratulations, you have completed the CEO prompt. Go to page 96.

Financial Analyst

Basking in self-congratulations after batting away countless bugs, your solo-architected stock guru finally shows uncanny prowess across markets...at first. Soon however, a wayward glitch triggers catastrophic cascading trades exceeding safeguards.

Over minutes your rogue AI hemorrhages $10 million from stunned clients expecting perfection - not apparent madness from the machine you birthed and vouched for alone. As higher-ups burst in demanding answers, all you can bleat is "I don't understand what went wrong!"

As emergency meetings drag late, dread magnifies at the towering house of cards now wobbling over your credibility. By sunrise, frantic damage control fails to regain trust in systems built on a foundation of fragile overconfidence.

Within weeks, crestfallen and disgraced you're forced to resign, becoming the case study on ambition blind to the exponential perils of playing solo AI god. The moral's clear: seeking outside wisdom when dicing with danger shows strength - not weakness. Your now humbled replacement certainly agrees, building safety nets around once unfettered machine learning fiefdoms.

Congratulations, you have completed the Financial Analyst prompt. Return to page 6 to begin the Medical Research prompt.

CEO

After trials optimizing fashion and meetings through GenAI prove profoundly successful, insatiable curiosity takes hold to explore its limits. Soon you discreetly delegate administrative tediums like finance reports or sales forecasts to your algorithmic assistant.

As once crushing responsibilities vanish, you walk taller with renewed vigor to personally champion innovative visions for shaping the company's future. Even the most challenging leadership meetings now feel effortless, decisions anchored by machine-learned wisdom subtly whispered discreetly through a wireless earpiece linked to your AI advisor.

At the next executive summit you single out young Sara for their pioneering advocacy. You commission a skills inventory of where modern GenAI can amplify output. Presenting this guidebook company-wide, you encourage employees to embrace augmentations that feel aligned rather than threatening.

Within months, productivity surges into record peaks as workers harmonize carbon talent with silicon enhancements.

Congratulations, you have completed the CEO prompt. Go to page 96.

Medical Research

Seeking relief, you allow a cutting-edge GenAI to generate analysis summaries after carefully redacting sensitive information, upholding security measures requiring human eyes only to view certain datasets. Despite limited visibility, the GenAI still yields valuable insights into drug viability.

However, with crucial statistics still under lock and key, analysis remains critically incomplete. Yet restoring efficiency tempts secrecy shortcuts...

Do you:

Option 1: Succumb and allow the AI full data access once more, directly injecting the redacted stats back into its system for convenient yet policy-skirting comprehensiveness. *Go to Page 69*

Option 2: Manually reincorporate the statistics yourself, retaining oversight over sensitive data that only trusted researchers can touch under strict protocols. Accuracy resumes with principled patience. *Go to Page 93*

Code Development

Recognizing AI's limitations in identifying subtle security flaws, you call upon your ace programming squad to address the system bugs flagged by the algorithm. Through days and nights, your combined human-AI cyber defense team isolates and patches every hole. Guided by silicon insights but grounded in carbon intuition, the strengthened code evolves into a formidable digital fortress.

As the deadline arrives, the intrusion system ships to an eagerly awaiting Third National. Mere weeks later, its newly hardened defenses detect and neutralize an onslaught of hacking attempts targeting vulnerabilities only human eyes could have located. Third National execs are thrilled at their impermeable cyber shield. "Fantastic work...your team makes an unbeatable AI-assisted security combo," they applaud. Word of your successful blend of human diligence and machine learning quickly spreads.

Your reputation soars as CS Solutions' becomes the go-to for financial institutions demanding both security and cutting-edge innovation. Your proud boss claps you on the back. "Keep up the good work leveraging GenAI as a tool rather than replacement for humans. That's the future of technology and I you'll lead us right to it!"

Congratulations, you have completed the Code Development prompt. Return to page 2 to begin the Job Hunt prompt.

Medical Research

Determined to balance security with efficiency, you carefully reincorporate the crucial redacted data yourself rather than blindly entrusting it to algorithms. The finished report shines as your magnum opus, reflecting meticulous analysis sharpened by GenAI collaboration.

When you unveil the hybrid document, awestruck leaders describe it as utterly remarkable. But upon hearing of the supporting AI role, smiles yield to furrowed brows emphasizing untested risks of premature automation.

"While the accomplishments here are laudable, we cannot sacrifice data controls in our AI zeal," they warn. "Until we implement comprehensive governance, manual oversight of sensitive datasets shall remain mandatory."

And yet promise glimmers amidst prudence - they invite you to spearhead an emerging GenAI ethics taskforce, recognizing that your vision behind the monitor, tempered with patience, may one day elevate all through equality of carbon and silicon minds.

Congratulations, you have completed the Medical Research prompt. Return to page 7 to begin the HR Manager prompt.

Professor

Though the AI proves adept at crafting rigorous exam questions, only human insight can judge the subjective nuances in students' handwritten struggles toward truth. So you diligently grade their work yourself, affirming algorithmic parity with previous semesters.

Emboldened by this harmony, you continue judiciously integrating automation to enrich learning. GenAI soon analyzes real-time feedback allowing personalized guidance. Another streamlines administrative tasks like scheduling, freeing more time for the rewards of human connection.

As experiments stack successes, you publish your methods and lead faculty workshops on mindfully navigating AI. Adoption accelerates, though some traditionalists whisper. But most rejoice at transcending either/or stereotypes to embrace the best of both worlds - tradition and transformation, wisdom and wonder hand in hand.

Congratulations, you have completed the Professor prompt. Return to page 5 to begin the Financial Analyst prompt.

The End

Congratulations on completing this hands-on guide charting GenAI's monumental impacts across diverse professional landscapes!

Through ten crucible scenarios, you navigated high-stakes decisions balancing opportunities and risks when collaborating with transformative algorithms. Mastering this delicate human-AI synthesis prepared you to steward future workflows blending automation with human accountability.

While the journey forward remains filled with complexities, take pride in emerging better equipped to prompt promising new adventures through principled AI integration. Your wisdom now joins a growing community plantation cultivating collaborative understanding between carbon and silicon minds.

By engaging with these very real tensions on the frontier, your perspective becomes ever more essential to collectively constructing an equitable path ahead. Our shared future will rely on compassionate competency from pioneers like yourself guiding boardrooms and beyond with care, creativity, and courage. Onward!